Groundwood Books / House of Anansi Press
groundwoodbooks.com

We acknowledge for their financial support of our publishing program the Canada
Council for the Arts, the Ontario Arts Council and the Government of Canada.

Canada Council Conseil des Arts
for the Arts du Canada

ONTARIO ARTS COUNCIL
CONSEIL DES ARTS DE L'ONTARIO
an Ontario government agency
un organisme du gouvernement de l'Ontario

With the participation of the Government of Canada
Avec la participation du gouvernement du Canada | Canada

Library and Archives Canada Cataloguing in Publication
Thornhill, Jan, author, illustrator
The triumphant tale of the house sparrow / Jan Thornhill.
Issued in print and electronic formats.
ISBN 978-1-77306-006-4 (hardcover). —ISBN 978-1-77306-007-1 (PDF)
1. House sparrow—Juvenile literature. 2. Introduced birds—
Juvenile literature. I. Title. II. Title: House sparrow.
QL696.P264T46 2018   j598.8'87   C2017-905297-7
                    C2017-905298-5

The illustrations for this book were created digitally.
Design by Michael Solomon
Printed and bound in Malaysia

MIX
Paper from
responsible sources
FSC
www.fsc.org   FSC® C012700

THE TRIUMPHANT TALE *of the*
HOUSE
SPARROW

JAN THORNHILL

GROUNDWOOD BOOKS
HOUSE OF ANANSI PRESS
TORONTO   BERKELEY

BEHOLD THE MOST despised bird in human history!

You know the one. It's that small brown bird that boldly hops about on sidewalks pecking at dried-up bits of hot-dog bun. The one that chirps monotonously, and loudly, outside your bedroom window. The one you sometimes see flying around inside airports or shopping malls. Yes, that one — the House Sparrow.

For more than ten thousand years, this bird has lived alongside us and nowhere else. And for just as long, we have tried to get rid of it. Yet worldwide, at least half a billion House Sparrows still survive.

So why is it not yet extinct, like the Passenger Pigeon or the Great Auk?

Part of the answer is that the House Sparrow has always been — like us — one of the most adaptable creatures on Earth.

Long, long ago — in prehistoric times — there was another kind of sparrow that lived in the Middle East. Like other birds, this one nested in the wild. It also migrated every year.

Then, around twelve thousand years ago, something in its neighborhood changed. The mammal that walked upright stopped roaming around, and — wonder of wonders! — it started growing the sparrow's favorite food. Grain.

The early sparrow quickly changed its habits. It began building its nests in cavities in human shelters instead of in trees, near the fields of wheat and oats that people were now cultivating. With such plentiful food, the sparrow no longer needed to migrate. Soon it lost the knack for long-distance flying altogether and rarely ventured more than a couple of miles from where it had hatched — places that were now always near humans.

It had become the House Sparrow.

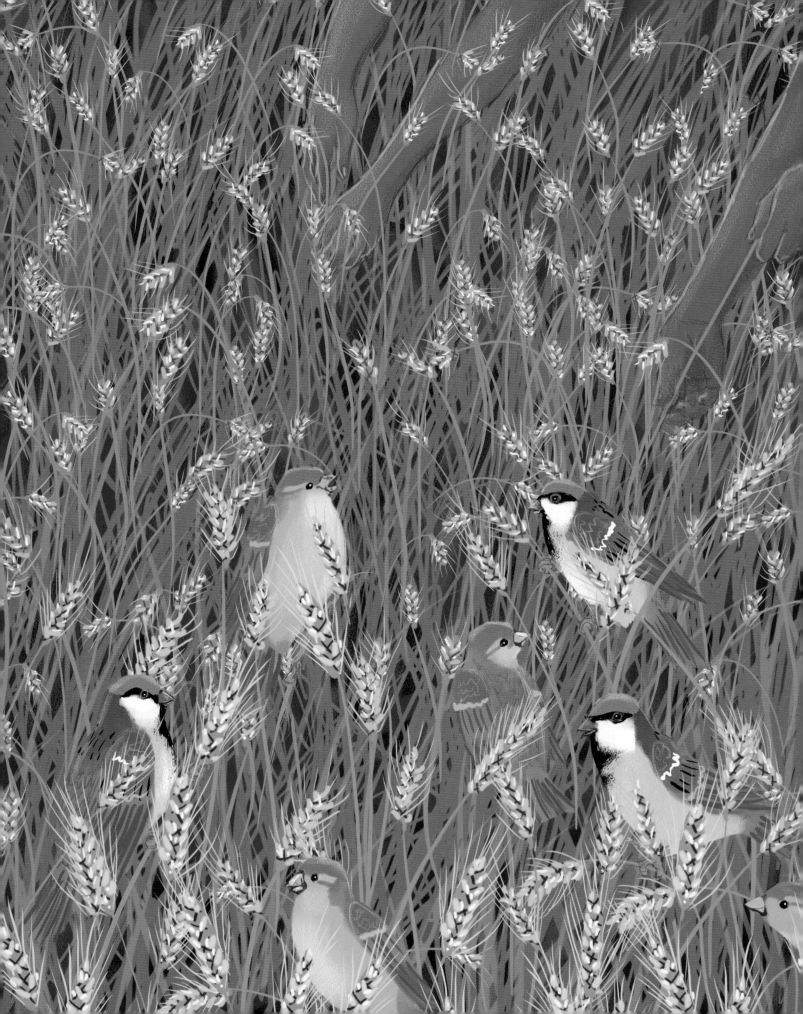

The early House Sparrow built a bulky, messy nest out of dried grasses and weeds, lined with soft feathers. It builds the same kind of nest today, though now it often includes modern materials, such as nylon string, shreds of paper and plastic — even bits of stuffing pulled from discarded armchairs.

The male and female build the nest together, usually in a crevice or hole. An average of five off-white eggs are laid, each splattered with brown dots and dashes. Both parents take turns keeping the eggs warm and, when they hatch, both parents feed the chicks.

For the first few days of their lives, the nestlings are offered a constant supply of insects. The parents then switch to feeding them the same vegetarian diet as their own — grains and other seeds, as well as flowers, fruits, buds, and scraps we throw away.

A week or so after the chicks leave the nest, the parents turn their backs on them. The female returns to the nest and lays another clutch of eggs. When this second brood is independent, the male and female start all over again. Sometimes, if the weather stays warm, they'll raise a fourth brood, or even a fifth!

So, not only is the House Sparrow adaptable — if there's lots to eat, it can multiply quickly.

And its most important food is also ours — the grass seeds we call grain.

As agriculture spread from the Middle East into India, North Africa and Europe, so, too, did the House Sparrow.

Over the centuries, tiny clusters of farms grew into villages, villages grew into towns, towns swelled into cities. The House Sparrow quickly adapted to each new human environment, where it could always find nesting cavities in buildings, plenty of grain, and insects to feed its hatchlings.

Except when caring for its young, the House Sparrow socializes, feeds and roosts in small flocks. At the end of the nesting season, it gathers into much larger flocks that can raid fields and orchards. Ten or twenty sparrows can't do much damage. But hundreds? Thousands?

We humans have never been very good at sharing the food we grow with other animals — unless those animals are pets or livestock. The ones that eat our crops, we consider pests … and we always have.

Long before the Great Pyramid was built, the Ancient Egyptians were using a hieroglyph of a House Sparrow to describe something as "bad" or "evil." So even that far back the bird must have been an agricultural pest. The Egyptians were expert bird-netters, though, and they would have caught large numbers in grain fields and nighttime roosts.

What did they do with all the sparrows they caught?

A clue lies inside a two-thousand-year-old falcon mummy. Scans have shown the remains of a House Sparrow in its stomach.

For centuries, mummified falcons, cats, crocodiles, ibises and other animals were purchased by Egyptians to offer to their gods in return for favors. So many of these animals were mummified — millions have been found — that they must have been raised for the purpose. And what better food for a captive cat or falcon than a common, fast-breeding field pest like the House Sparrow?

By 50 BC, the House Sparrow ranged from the foothills of the Himalayas, to the Sahara, to the fjords of Scandinavia and everywhere in between. But the British Isles were still sparrow-free. The English Channel was just too vast an expanse of water for such a poor long-distance flyer. Ever adaptable, though, the House Sparrow found an easier way to get there. It traveled as a stowaway on ships — ships carrying legions of Roman soldiers.

Along with other supplies, each Roman legionnaire had to carry his own rations of wheat and barley, which he would grind into flour to make porridge, pancakes or flatbread. Horses also ate rations of grain, usually oats. Both on ship and off, the House Sparrow simply hopped between the feet of soldiers and horses, pecking up spilled grain, crusts of bread and other scraps.

The House Sparrow followed the conquering army through Britain, breeding and multiplying along the way. By the time the Romans packed up and left four hundred years later, the tiny bird had conquered a much greater area than the most powerful army on Earth.

Everywhere the House Sparrow settled it multiplied so quickly that it just as quickly became a pest.

People caught it with nets and traps and poles tipped with sticky sap. Young boys armed with noisy wooden clappers were paid to make such a racket in grain fields that sparrows were afraid to land. "Sparrow catcher" became an actual job.

To keep sparrows out of their thatched roofs, peasants hung clay nesting pots from their eaves. Before the young raised in these cozy pots could fledge, they were harvested for the cooking pot. There's not a lot of meat on a sparrow, so a single brood was not enough to make a meal. In fact, one old recipe for a simple sparrow pie calls for the meat from at least five dozen birds!

But despite these efforts to get rid of it, the House Sparrow continued to multiply and raid crops. By the 1700s, peasants in Germany were forced to deliver a set number of sparrow heads to authorities each year or pay a hefty fine. In other places, small bounties of a few pennies were paid to encourage people to catch them.

In England, records from the eighteenth and nineteenth centuries show that millions of bounties were paid. But barely a dent was made in the sparrow population. On the tiny Isle of Wight, for instance, though thousands of sparrows were trapped and netted every year, there was never a drop in the yearly catch!

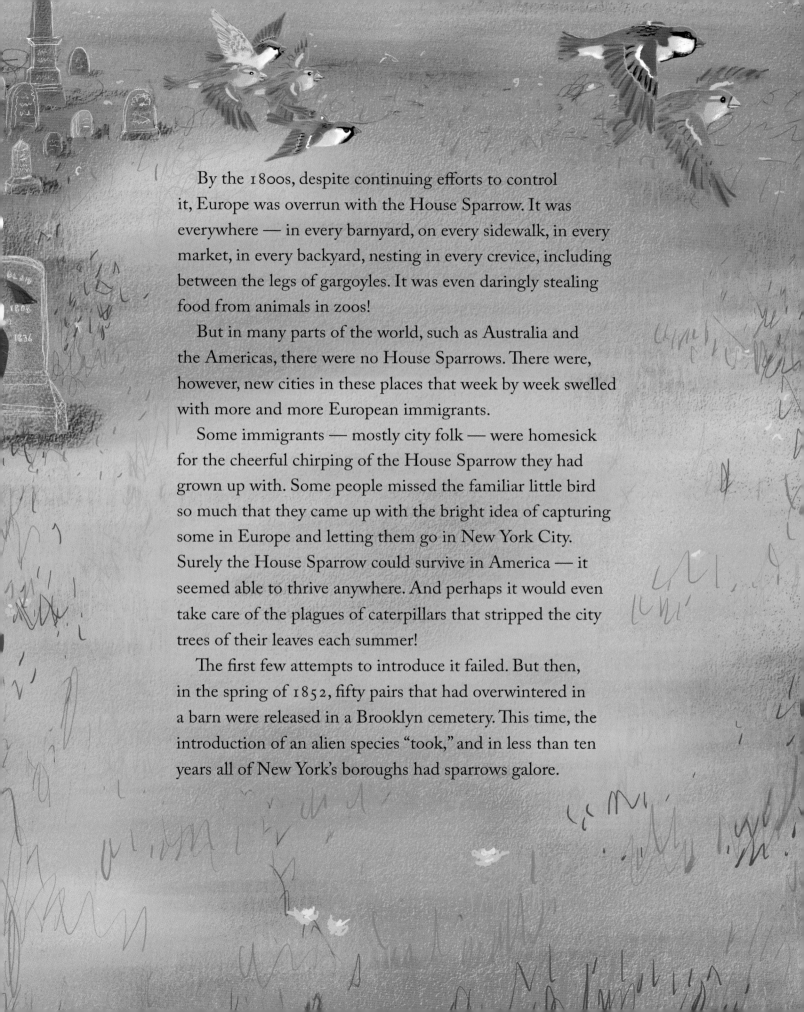

By the 1800s, despite continuing efforts to control it, Europe was overrun with the House Sparrow. It was everywhere — in every barnyard, on every sidewalk, in every market, in every backyard, nesting in every crevice, including between the legs of gargoyles. It was even daringly stealing food from animals in zoos!

But in many parts of the world, such as Australia and the Americas, there were no House Sparrows. There were, however, new cities in these places that week by week swelled with more and more European immigrants.

Some immigrants — mostly city folk — were homesick for the cheerful chirping of the House Sparrow they had grown up with. Some people missed the familiar little bird so much that they came up with the bright idea of capturing some in Europe and letting them go in New York City. Surely the House Sparrow could survive in America — it seemed able to thrive anywhere. And perhaps it would even take care of the plagues of caterpillars that stripped the city trees of their leaves each summer!

The first few attempts to introduce it failed. But then, in the spring of 1852, fifty pairs that had overwintered in a barn were released in a Brooklyn cemetery. This time, the introduction of an alien species "took," and in less than ten years all of New York's boroughs had sparrows galore.

People in other American cities wanted the House Sparrow, too, so they brought in their own breeding populations, or got birds from New York. Conditions in America were so perfect for the House Sparrow that it had no problem raising one brood after another wherever it was introduced.

And so it multiplied. And multiplied. And multiplied. And spread. Some even hitched train rides across the country alongside livestock!

Grain was plentiful everywhere, largely because horses
were everywhere. On farms and in towns and cities, the
House Sparrow snapped up every oat that spilled from a
feed bag. It even pecked undigested grain from manure! And
though it turned its beak up at tree-stripping caterpillars,
there was no shortage of tastier insects to feed its young.
Better still, unlike native birds, the House Sparrow was
already comfortable living near people, so it had little
competition in towns and cities for nesting sites and food.

Basically, America was House Sparrow heaven.

At least, it was for a while.

At first, everyone was delighted. It was just so grand to live in cities enlivened by such a familiar and entertaining bird! In several parks, elaborate sparrow "apartment buildings" were even built to encourage it to breed so there would be lots of sparrows for people to enjoy.

In less than twenty years, though, it became difficult to find a park bench anywhere that wasn't whitewashed with sparrow droppings. The din at dawn when thousands of sparrows started chirping, and in the evening before they settled down for the night, was deafening.

The House Sparrow was also a bully. On the edges of towns and on farmsteads, it stole feed from chickens and drove away native birds. And in farm fields it did what it had always done. It attacked crops.

A battle cry arose. The House Sparrow had to be stopped!

Pros and cons appeared in newspapers across the land. Name calling began. The House Sparrow was called a villain, a cuss, a disreputable character, a glutton and a parasite. It was impudent, insolent, irascible, irritable, intolerable and lazy. It even caused fires! In Pittsburgh, it lined its nests with fluff from the cotton mill that ignited when sparks from the iron mill landed on them.

But wait! said others. They're so cheerful, so frolicsome, so amusing! And the children so love them! More importantly, what would happen if they didn't eat the seeds of weeds and feed their nestlings insect pests like grasshoppers, caterpillars and beetles?

The American Sparrow Wars had begun.

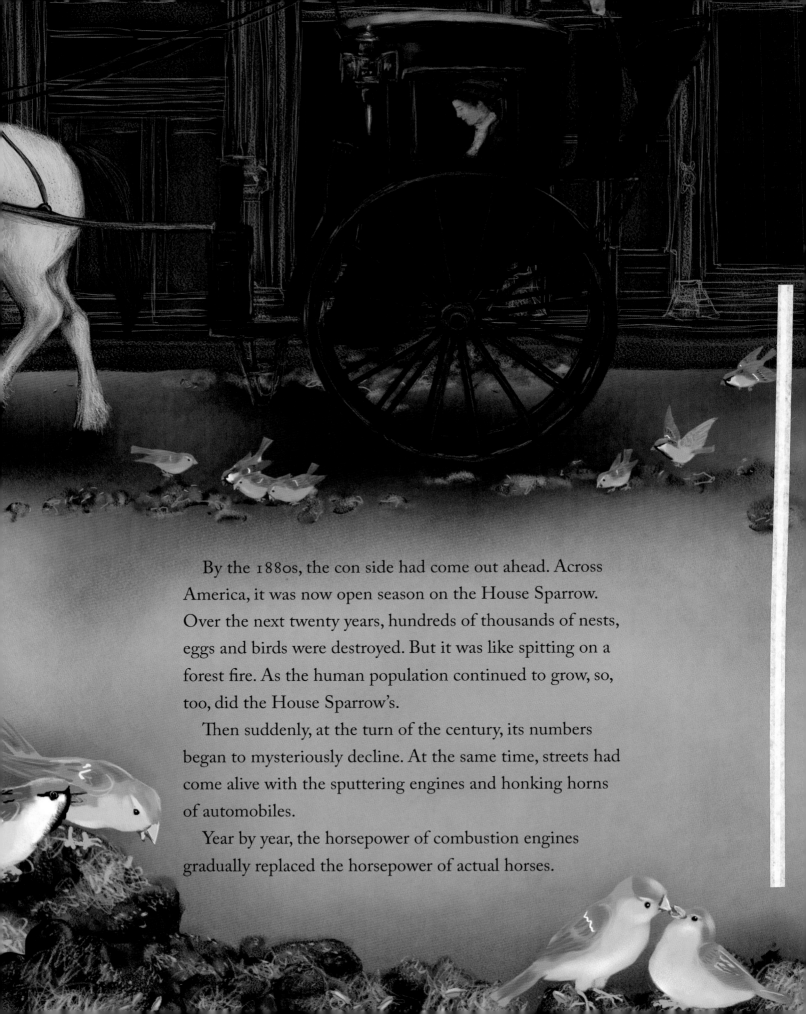

By the 1880s, the con side had come out ahead. Across
America, it was now open season on the House Sparrow.
Over the next twenty years, hundreds of thousands of nests,
eggs and birds were destroyed. But it was like spitting on a
forest fire. As the human population continued to grow, so,
too, did the House Sparrow's.

Then suddenly, at the turn of the century, its numbers
began to mysteriously decline. At the same time, streets had
come alive with the sputtering engines and honking horns
of automobiles.

Year by year, the horsepower of combustion engines
gradually replaced the horsepower of actual horses.

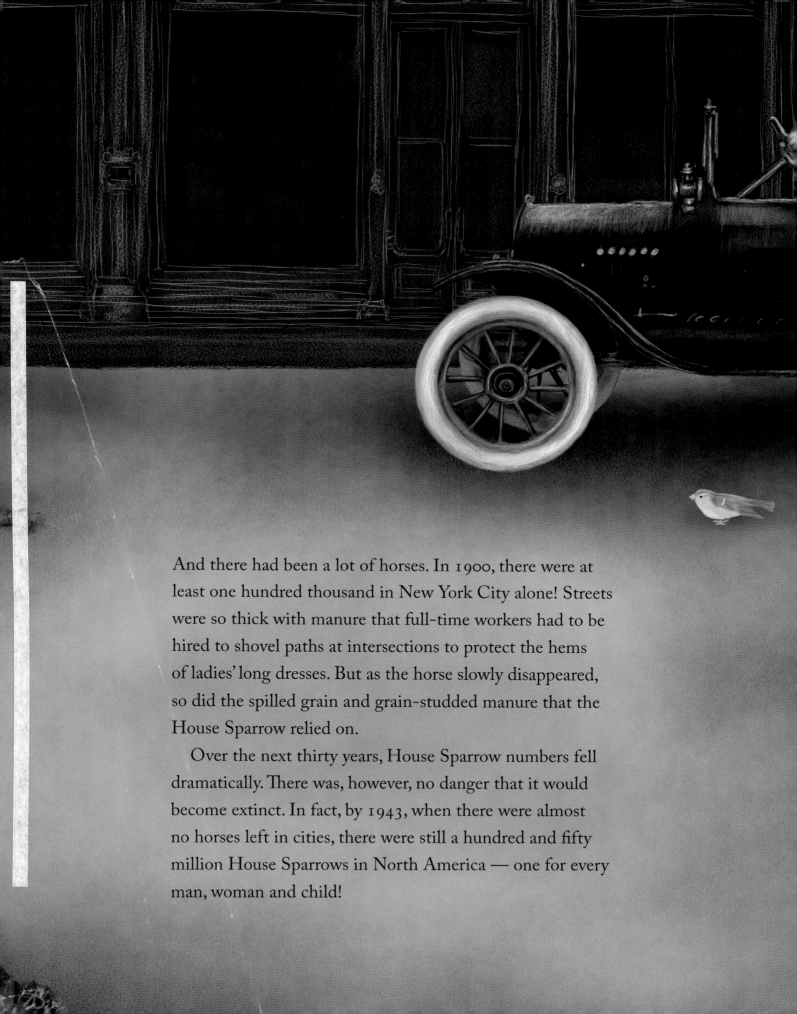

And there had been a lot of horses. In 1900, there were at least one hundred thousand in New York City alone! Streets were so thick with manure that full-time workers had to be hired to shovel paths at intersections to protect the hems of ladies' long dresses. But as the horse slowly disappeared, so did the spilled grain and grain-studded manure that the House Sparrow relied on.

Over the next thirty years, House Sparrow numbers fell dramatically. There was, however, no danger that it would become extinct. In fact, by 1943, when there were almost no horses left in cities, there were still a hundred and fifty million House Sparrows in North America — one for every man, woman and child!

The House Sparrow is not the only sparrow that lives — and thrives — alongside humans.

About ten thousand years ago, in China, another sparrow began living near the first rice farmers. Like its cousin, the House Sparrow, this eastern one evolved to live with people, eating the grains they grew and nesting in nearby trees or under eaves and in holes in their homes. The Eurasian Tree Sparrow had arrived.

The House Sparrow and Eurasian Tree Sparrow are closely related, so it's not surprising that their behaviors, tastes and life histories are a lot alike. The Eurasian Tree Sparrow also spread in exactly the same way as the House Sparrow, by following the expansion of agriculture. And, just like the House Sparrow, it multiplied and multiplied and multiplied.

It also attacked crops.

By 1958, there were so many Eurasian Tree Sparrows in
China that the country's leader, Chairman Mao, declared war
on them. He had calculated how many more human mouths
could be fed if there were no sparrows. To him, it was obvious
— China didn't need such a greedy species. Scientists tried
to warn him of what might happen if there were no Eurasian
Tree Sparrows to control insect pests. Mao didn't listen.

Instead, he told his people to kill every sparrow they saw.
Special days were chosen and everyone stayed home from
work and school. Young and old alike rose before dawn
and left their homes carrying anything that could make
noise. From sunrise to sunset, everyone blew horns, clanged
cymbals and banged on drums, gongs, washbasins, and pots

and pans. The skittish sparrows tried to escape, but wherever they turned there were more people making noise. The birds were too frightened to land. Instead, they dropped, exhausted, from the sky.

It's possible that a billion sparrows died that year.

And the scientists were right. Plagues of insects unlike anything ever seen before decimated crops across the land. By the end of the year, there was not enough food for China's growing population. In less than three years, more than thirty million people starved to death. Though the destruction of the Eurasian Tree Sparrow was not the sole cause of this catastrophe, it was likely a major contribution.

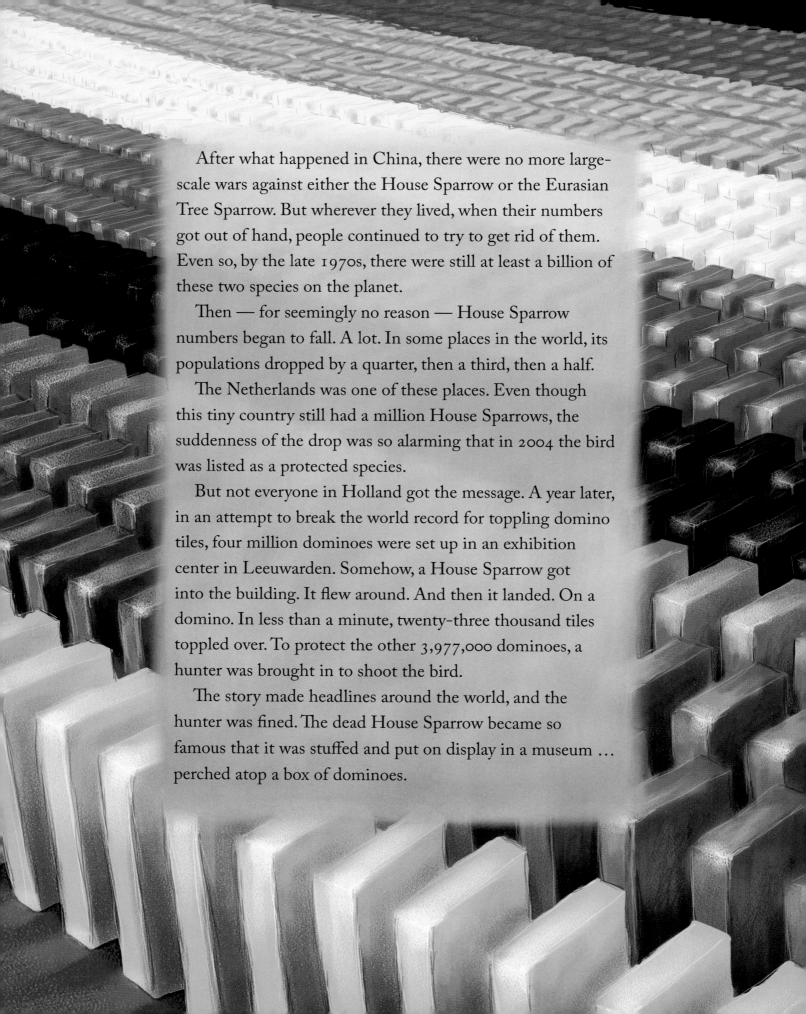

After what happened in China, there were no more large-scale wars against either the House Sparrow or the Eurasian Tree Sparrow. But wherever they lived, when their numbers got out of hand, people continued to try to get rid of them. Even so, by the late 1970s, there were still at least a billion of these two species on the planet.

Then — for seemingly no reason — House Sparrow numbers began to fall. A lot. In some places in the world, its populations dropped by a quarter, then a third, then a half.

The Netherlands was one of these places. Even though this tiny country still had a million House Sparrows, the suddenness of the drop was so alarming that in 2004 the bird was listed as a protected species.

But not everyone in Holland got the message. A year later, in an attempt to break the world record for toppling domino tiles, four million dominoes were set up in an exhibition center in Leeuwarden. Somehow, a House Sparrow got into the building. It flew around. And then it landed. On a domino. In less than a minute, twenty-three thousand tiles toppled over. To protect the other 3,977,000 dominoes, a hunter was brought in to shoot the bird.

The story made headlines around the world, and the hunter was fined. The dead House Sparrow became so famous that it was stuffed and put on display in a museum … perched atop a box of dominoes.

When bird populations crash so quickly, it usually means that most of the young are not living long enough to breed. Why might this have happened to the House Sparrow? What has changed so drastically in such a short time?

We have.

All over the world, we have changed our homes. Old-style thatched and curved-tile roofs have always been favored nesting sites for the House Sparrow. But these materials have been replaced with modern steel roofing and flat shingles. To save energy, we have also begun to fill in every nook and cranny in old buildings. New buildings have no holes at all.

In many neighborhoods, there are fewer trees, hedges and ivy-covered walls, where the House Sparrow likes to roost at night. Cities have fewer gardens to supply insects for nestlings, and there are fewer vacant lots to supply weed seeds.

We have also changed the way we farm. To produce more and more food for growing human populations, we poison weeds before they have a chance to make seeds. We also poison insects. Grain is now grown in vast expanses far from the House Sparrow's urban nesting sites and nighttime roosts. And we harvest, transport and store this grain so efficiently that almost none is left behind or spilled.

We also have more domestic cats than ever before, and we use cellphones that rely on towers that emit radiation, which might affect the House Sparrow's ability to navigate and catch food.

To top it all off, it used to be common for people to use tablecloths at every meal — and at the end of every meal, they'd shake off the crumbs outdoors. When was the last time *you* saw someone shaking a sparrow's meal off a tablecloth?

In North America, House Sparrow numbers have dropped so much in some communities that it has become hard to find. But — unlike in Europe and India — in North America, no alarm has been sounded. The plight of the polar bear — an animal that few have seen in the wild — is constantly in the news. But a sudden crash in populations of a bird that is so common you hardly even notice it? No one seems to care.

This is partly because many people believe the House Sparrow should never have been brought to North America in the first place. They consider it an invasive species. Invasive species are plants or animals that have been introduced into new environments. They usually spread and multiply quickly, often competing with native species for breeding sites or food. It can be extremely difficult to control them — and expensive.

Unquestionably, the House Sparrow is a feisty competitor. Because it lives year-round in the same area, it usually gets first dibs on nesting boxes in the spring, even those boxes meant for native species. If a bluebird, Tree Swallow or other hole-nesting species is lucky enough to snag a nesting box first, the House Sparrow will push out the eggs or nestlings. It has even been known to kill adult birds.

But wait a second! Was the House Sparrow actually
released into a new environment when it was brought to
North America? Isn't its environment the same as our
environment — the cities and towns we build?

Before there were electronic sensors to detect odorless
gases, miners took caged canaries with them underground.
If a buildup of dangerous gases occurred, a canary would
sway drunkenly on its perch, or fall off, and the miners would
know to evacuate.

Because the House Sparrow normally lives its whole life in a very small area, it can be a living indicator of pollutants in that place. To scientists, it is just like a canary in a coal mine — except the coal mine is our urban environment.

Since the House Sparrow lives where we live, wouldn't it be smart to figure out why it's disappearing? What if the culprit is something that is as unhealthy for humans as it is for the House Sparrow?

Though we still don't know what has been causing House Sparrow populations to decline, there's some good news. In the Netherlands, and in England, the decline appears to be leveling out. Perhaps in these places more people are welcoming the House Sparrow to bird feeders, or they're providing more birdhouses for it to nest in. Or maybe it has simply begun to adapt to our newfangled modern ways.

The House Sparrow is, after all, adaptable. For ten thousand years, it has changed as we have changed. It has followed us around the planet, and can be found on every continent except Antarctica.

It has built its nests in medieval churches, in the rigging of ships sailing the high seas, and in coal mines deep below the ground (where it shared grain with pit ponies). More recently, it has nested in traffic lights, in store-sign letters and even in outdoor barbecues.

It has learned to stay up after dark to catch insects attracted by artificial lights. It has discovered that it can control the parasites that trouble its young by adding nicotine-laden cigarette butts to its nests. It has even learned how to open doors.

All over the world, the House Sparrow flies in and out of grocery stores, airports and other buildings that offer food and shelter. All it has to do is flutter in front of the motion sensors of automatic doors to trigger them. Then — *voilà!* — like magic, the doors whoosh open.

If any animal is adaptable enough to survive in our fast–changing human environment, it is the House Sparrow.

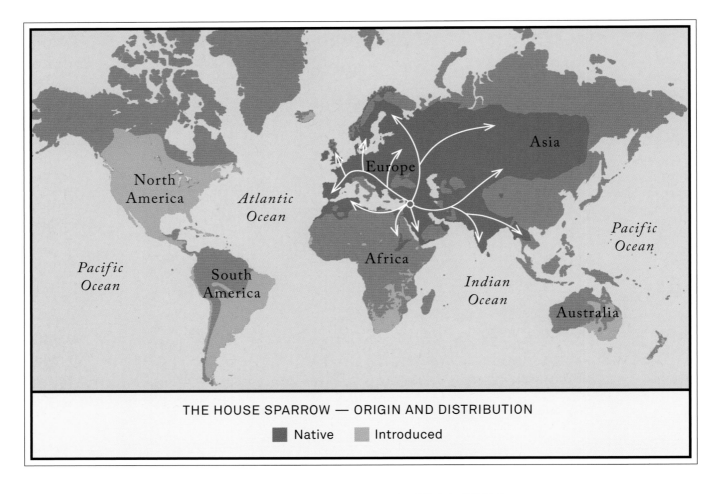

THE HOUSE SPARROW — ORIGIN AND DISTRIBUTION

■ Native ■ Introduced

THE LIFE CYCLE OF THE HOUSE SPARROW

1
The male and female mate for life. They build a nest together.

2
The female lays between four and seven eggs. She spends more time than the male keeping them warm.

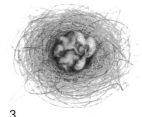

3
After about twelve days, the eggs hatch. The chicks open their eyes four days later and gradually grow feathers.

4
Fifteen to seventeen days after hatching, the fledglings leave the nest, flying for the first time.

5
The parents feed their young for another week or so, and then the female returns to the nest to lay more eggs.

6
A year later the young birds choose mates and build a nest together.

GLOSSARY

brood – the young of a bird hatched at one time

cavity – an unfilled space within a solid object

clutch – a single nest of eggs

combustion engine – an engine that generates power by burning fuel

fjord – a long, narrow inlet bordered by steep cliffs

fledgling – a young bird whose feathers are large enough for flight

gargoyle – a grotesque human or animal carving with a water-spout mouth

hieroglyph – a written character that looks like a picture

invasive – describes something that spreads or grows where you don't want it

legion – the Roman army unit of 3,000 to 6,000 men

navigate – to accurately find one's way

preening – (of a bird) using its beak to straighten and clean its feathers

radiation – energy that is transmitted in waves or particles

roost – a place where birds rest or sleep; also, to sit or sleep

WILD ANIMALS THAT CHOOSE TO LIVE WITH US

The House Sparrow is not the only wild animal that has adapted to humans and human activities. Numerous other species all over the world thrive in human environments. It's not that they can't survive without us — life is just so much easier with us. We provide these animals with shelter. And we protect them from predators. But the biggest draw is usually connected to … food.

All over the world, multitudes of animals feast on insects attracted to our artificial lights, raid our kitchen cupboards, gorge on our garbage and even drink our blood (think mosquitoes!). Some of their adaptations are astonishing. Crows in Japan, for instance, have figured out how to use passing cars as giant nutcrackers. Not only that, but some crows now place the nuts they want cracked on crosswalks, so the nut meat can be safely retrieved when oncoming traffic stops!

If you look up the animals in the following list — or, better yet, observe the ones that live near you — you will find that, like the House Sparrow, each of these species has its own fascinating tale to tell.

Bats (worldwide)

Bedbugs (worldwide)

Canada Goose (North America, Europe, New Zealand)

Centipedes (worldwide)

Clothing Moth (worldwide)

Cockroaches (worldwide)

Coyote (North America)

Crows, Ravens, Jays and Magpies (worldwide)

Fleas (worldwide)

Gulls (worldwide)

Head Louse (worldwide)

House Fly (worldwide)

House Gecko (warm parts of the world)

House Mouse (worldwide)

London Underground Mosquito (England)

Macaques (South Asia)

Mallard (North America, Europe)

Nine-banded Armadillo (North America)

Norway Rat (worldwide)

Pavement Ant (North America, Europe)

Peregrine Falcon (North America)

Rabbits (worldwide)

Common Raccoon (North America, Europe, Japan)

Red Fox (North America, Europe, Japan, Australia)

Red-tailed Hawk (North America)

Rock Dove/Pigeon (worldwide)

Silverfish (worldwide)

Spiders (worldwide)

Squirrels (North America, Europe, Asia)

Virginia Opossum (North America)

Wild Boar (Berlin)